The Many Sides of

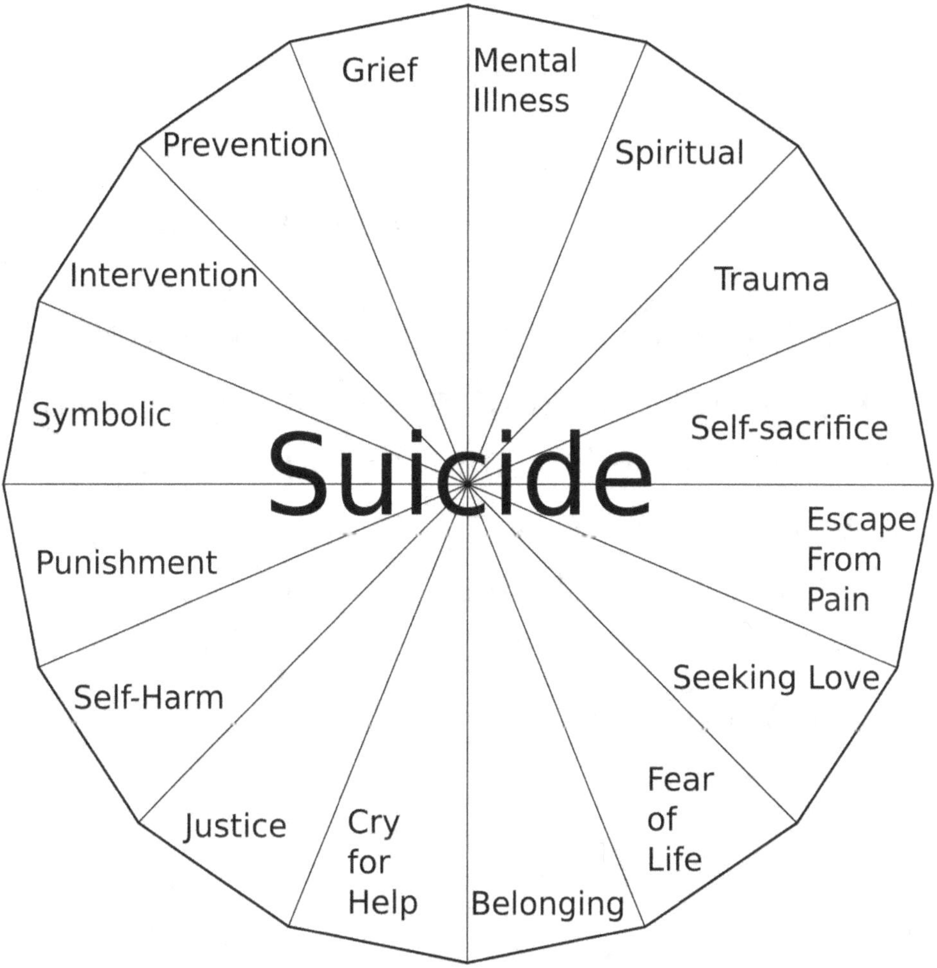

Judena Klebs

Dedication

I dedicate this book to my therapist, Mackenzie Sainz and to all those who, like her, are eager to help the suicidal person.

Preface

For many years I have been observing a great lack of understanding about suicide. As I struggled with my own chronic suicidal temptations and also watched others struggle, both inside and outside mental hospitals, I looked for resources and read many books on the subject, seeking help.
Most of the books I came across were very inadequate to explain the subject or to help a suicidal person overcome their tendencies and many were detrimental to me and to others. The majority of these books were very judgmental and would attempt to either scare someone out of suicide or to shame them for even thinking about it. Several Christian authors claim that you could never be forgiven by God if you tried to take your own life. One of the books I read claimed that depression, itself, is caused by the "sin" of self-pity.
It has been a strong burden on my heart and mind to write a book that will address this subject in a way that is helpful to both the suicidal person and to those who want to help them. I also hope to help unravel a subject that is more complicated than it has been treated in the past.
I have noticed that many people try to simplify this problem as having only one cause or only one solution. It is much more complicated than that, which is what I hope to show through these pages as well as to provide some real answers.

Introduction

In this book, I have identified 16 different aspects of suicide which need to be addressed and clarified separately, This is because, through the years, I personally struggled with this problem and in searching for and examining possible solutions to it, I noticed that most people dealt with it in such a simplified way.
The problem of suicide is complex and its various solutions are many. This is why I break it apart and examine it the way I do in these pages. The more educated we all become about this subject, the more we can prevent tragedy and save lives.

All of the stories I share in this book are either exactly true as told or are based on true experiences of people. However, I changed most of the names. The only names I did not change are the name of my son, Chandler, who writes openly about his own struggles in his own books, and of course, my own name as I share my own struggles, which I tell about in the first person as I refer to them.

Chapter 1   The Mental Illness Side

Major Depression

Gina was experiencing a deep sadness. It overtook her mind and thoughts of suicide overwhelmed her. Of course, she wished she could be happy but nothing about her life felt right to her and she was always on the verge of tears.

People would tell Gina to "cheer up" or say, "Happiness is a choice" or "Depression is a choice" or, "You would feel better if you would just smile and choose to be happy." They even told her they felt sorry for her husband having to live with a depressed person and "Count your blessings and stop feeling sorry for yourself".

How hard Gina tried to come out of these terrible feelings! But nothing worked. She could only wonder if death was the only thing that would bring her relief.

But, did she really want to die? She was afraid of death, too, but feeling so bad all the time had to be worse than death, she thought. She just felt she could not go on living. Gina also knew that if she told anyone about her thoughts of suicide, they would judge her and tell her what a terrible sin it would be and that God would punish her in hell. Her church friends would try to get her to repent of this wicked thought. Where could she find help and relief?

Gina was suffering from Major Depression. a disease of the brain. It is not simply a bad mood. It is an illness. Scientists have discovered chemical imbalances in the brain which can cause these symptoms. Psychiatrists have learned how to successfully treat Major Depression with medicine and other therapies. Gina and others like her can receive help in overcoming depression, not through will-power but through the assistance of Mental Health professionals.

Depression can cause the brain to "freeze" with a type of paralysis focused on suicidal thoughts. No amount of self-effort can rescue a person from depression's dark pit of despair. But cooperating with the treatment of mental health professionals can bring healing and rehabilitation. Major Depression needs to be treated like the illness that it is, just like any other illness rather than putting shame on the person experiencing it.

Bi-Polar Disorder

Steven had big mood swings. He would go through days or even sometimes weeks, hardly sleeping, talking and thinking fast, feeling as though he could do anything. He would be in such a high, energetic mood and accomplish so much during this time. But then, suddenly, Steven would feel hopeless and sink into a deep depression in which he began to long for death. During these times, he would sometimes attempt suicide, leaving his family and friends stunned. Steven had "manic-depressive disorder" or now more commonly called, "Bi-Polar Illness". There are several variations of this illness, which tends to be hereditary. It is often treated with "mood stabilizers". Once again, Steven cannot just "snap out" of this cycle but needs treatment. It is a disease of the brain.

Schizophrenia

Diane was troubled by voices telling her how bad she was and that she should die. She felt afraid and suspicious of people which caused her to isolate from others. She thought about suicide often because she wanted to escape the awful fear she felt about all the voices and the scary things she saw that others seemed not to see.
People referred to Diane as crazy or possibly dangerous because she acted strangely and tended to stare at the people of whom she felt afraid. Diane was suffering from Schizophrenia, another illness of the brain which tends to be hereditary. Psychiatrists have learned to treat people with this illness with "anti-psychotic" medicines in order to help control its symptoms. This illness can also lead to suicide.

Other Disorders and Substance Abuse

There are other disorders which can lead to suicidal behavior such as Borderline Personality Disorder. Also substance abuse such as Alcoholism can lead to or aggravate suicidal tendencies with or without other mental illnesses present. Anxiety disorders can lead to suicide as well.
Postpartum Depression is another factor in some suicides. The hormonal changes after giving birth can affect the brain.
Mental Illness is a huge side to the suicidal spectrum. It is something which should be diagnosed and treated as soon as possible when a person struggles with suicide.

Chapter 2 The Spiritual Side

Spiritual Views

Debbie was an unhappy girl. She never seemed to be able to please her family. She would cry each night while trying to go to sleep. She felt so empty without her parent's affection. She had suffered abuse through the years and longed for some kind of nurturing and love to help heal the hurts inside of her.
Debbie's parents took her to church where they were prominent leaders and Sunday School teachers. They claimed to be "saved" and "sanctified" which meant they had attained "Christian Perfection". Often the preachers at Debbie's church would preach to the congregation about repenting of their sins so they could get "saved" from their sins and be able to go to heaven and not hell when they died. Also, the Christian hymns sung at church often included phrases such as, "I am happy since my burdens rolled away" and indicated that once a person is saved they are, "happy all the day". Debbie wished her burden of hurt would roll away. She thought she must not be saved and that meant she would go to hell when she died. When the preacher held an "altar call", inviting those who wanted to get saved to go to the front of the church and to kneel and pray at the altar, Debbie would often go. She would kneel at the altar, crying and begging God to save her. Her tears, which others assumed were tears of repentance from sin were really tears of hurt. Debbie had emotional problems which simply would not "roll away". She hoped she was saved but thought she must not be because she stayed so unhappy.
Many religions, including some of the churches of Christianity, don't take into account psychological and emotional realities. They often teach that depression and suicide are sins and that suicide is the "unpardonable sin". If this were true, even a suicide attempt would be unpardonable because it would be the same sin. However, the argument is sometimes made that a successful suicide attempt would be unpardonable because there is no time to repent once the person is dead.
The Bible, itself, does not actually condemn anyone for suicide. Judas, for example, was condemned for betraying Christ, not for his suicide. Samson is even listed in the "Hall of Faith" in Hebrews, chapter 11.

The Demonic Realm

Chris attended a Pentecostal Church. The leaders there taught about
miracles including deliverance from demons.
Chris had had a difficult background and had experienced abuse while
growing up. He had hated his abusers and remembered how the more he
hated them, the more a feeling of bondage would come over him. He also
had been depressed and suicidal throughout his life and had attempted
suicide several times.
As Chris was taught about the demonic realm, he realized there had
been spiritual battles going on inside of him, compelling him toward
suicide. Even though he had already dedicated his life to Christ, he
began to realize he needed deliverance from evil spirits which had
entered him through years of hatred.
The pastor and other members of the congregation prayed with him and
cast out several demons in the name of Jesus, starting with a "spirit
of suicide". This brought Chris some relief as he felt the demons leave and
felt less tormented afterwards. However, when later he would have
emotional struggles or thoughts of suicide, the pastor told him that he was
allowing the demon to return and that if he had been truly delivered,
he should be feeling happy.
Chris was feeling better but there was still so much hurt from the
abuse that had helped open the door to the demons to begin with, that
he could not be completely happy or free from emotional pain.
The spiritual world, as taught in many Pentecostal groups, is a
reality and the effectiveness of some exorcisms is evident. However,
not only are some "deliverance ministries" handled poorly but it is
often assumed that such things are a "cure-all".
If a person is still struggling with emotions and suicidal tendencies,
they are often blamed for "letting the devil" back into their lives.
Very often counseling and further emotional healing are needed.
The answer to this is to receive both spiritual and psychological
help. There is a real spiritual realm, of which many are not aware,
and I personally received help through a deliverance ministry in a
church. However, damage to the mind and emotions is also real and
needs to be addressed by mental health professionals. Perhaps this can be
illustrated by treatment required for a gunshot wound. The bullet needs to
be removed but the wound still needs healing.

Chapter 3 The Trauma Side

Abuse and Dissociative Identity Disorder

Julia had experienced trauma throughout her life. She had been abused as a child and gone through many frightening and shocking experiences even in adulthood. These caused her to experience Post Traumatic Stress Disorder (PTSD), which included flashbacks and nightmares. In order to cope with these experiences, Julia also developed "multiple personalities". These helped her to continue the task of growing up and to function in her adult world as well, by giving her other parts of herself to cope with the pain than the parts which must continue to function in other types of tasks. Some of these "personalities" or different parts of Julia were suicidal. They tried to escape her painful life through suicide and even tried to kill other parts of her that took the blame for things. Even though these different parts of Julia shared the same body, to Julia, this battle among her personalities was the only way she could cope with the conflicting roles she needed to play in order to maneuver through her life's tasks.

This brief explanation of Dissociative Identity Disorder and a poem called Many People is taken from my poetry book called From Rejection to Love:

Introduction to Many People:

There is a diagnosis called Dissociative Identity Disorder (D.I.D.), formerly known as Multiple Personality Disorder (M.P.D.). It is often misunderstood to be the result of demons or confused with other diagnoses.

Much of the breaking into different parts (often called Personalities) is due to trauma, especially in young childhood. Because the traumatic experiences are so great, in order to keep the mind sane, many times various parts of the mind manifest themselves separately. They are designated by the mind to carry certain memories and cope with them in their own way. Various other parts of the person may manifest themselves as helpers or they may be self-destructive in some way, sabotaging the work of healing and integration.

This poem expresses my experience with the struggle that goes on in the process of healing these various parts:

Many People

There are many people
Inside of me
Struggling and crying
And yearning to be free
All desperately searching
To find their way
All longing to see
A better day
They all carry pain
They all hold grief
Only by splitting
Can they find relief
Yet relief does not last
So they divide again
While each new part
Explodes with pain
These people overwhelm me
As they crowd into my soul
No one seems to understand
That they want to be whole
But they each must be healed
And work hand in hand
Building new dreams
Out of mountains of sand
The people who have struggled
To keep my mind alive
Have divided in my soul
To help me survive
They deserve honor
Not ridicule or shame
For they hold an identity
With or without a name
So help them heal
And comfort each one
Until they all shine together
Like rays of the sun

Suicidal personalities are often a part of D.I.D. They must be healed
and eventually integrated back into the whole person, fulfilling a
constructive role instead of a destructive one.

If you have had a lot of trauma in your life, it helps to find a therapist who is experienced in this area. One treatment which has proven to be effective in dealing with traumatic memories and which can sometimes assist with D.I.D integration is: Eye Movement Desensitization and Reprocessing (EMDR). I found that the healing of certain memories must take place in order for some of the personalities to integrate.

Chapter 4 The Self-Sacrifice Side

Jeremy always seemed to be in the way. No one had time for him and it
seemed that many people in his life thought he was a nuisance. He was
10 years old. His parents often complained that he was not helpful
enough and his older siblings just wanted him to leave them alone.
When Jeremy got a little bit older, he developed a disease which
crippled him. It was hard for his family to take care of him so he
felt as though he was even more of a burden.
Jeremy did not like himself. He became self-conscious about taking up
air and space that he thought only belonged to others. He decided to
commit suicide to get himself out of other's way. He felt as though
that was the most loving thing he could do.
After his suicide, everyone who knew Jeremy commented about how
selfish it was that Jeremy ended his life. They thought he should have
warned his family and not left so many unanswered questions behind
when he died.
Would there have been anyone to listen if Jeremy had tried to give
notice that he was feeling the need to get rid of himself for the sake
of others? Was anyone aware that he felt he was a burden?
One of the chief causes of suicide is the perception, whether accurate
or not, that one is a "burden". Many people perceive this because of
how they are treated by others or because they have a disability which
keeps them from contributing to others in a way significant to them or
that forces others to have to take care of them.
A sense of being a burden is a chief cause of suicide. One of the
important things to help a suicidal person want to live is to convince
them that they have significant things to contribute to the world.
I, personally, felt many times that I was taking up air and space in
this world that belonged to others. I thought that removing myself from
this world would be doing everyone a favor and freeing up the world
for those who deserved to live. My self-esteem needed to be built up to the
point in which I saw myself as a worthy contributor to the world. This is
key to off-setting the urge to make oneself a sacrifice for the sake of
others.

Chapter 5 The Escape from Pain Side

Chandler was in pain, both physically and emotionally. He had suffered sexual abuse at a very young age, which damaged his genitals and then, he suffered further damage to his testicles when he was older.
Besides all this, Chandler had Gender Dysphoria, a condition often caused by an odd number of sex chromosomes in someone who may be born one gender but who tends to identify as another. He began to call himself Chastity and think of himself as a girl.
Because of damage to her testicles, Chastity was in constant physical pain and, because she also was not interested in reproducing, she thought seriously about having her testicles removed. She proceeded to do research on this possibility.
After thoroughly investigating this option, Chastity tried to find a doctor who would be willing to perform an orchiectomy on her, the surgery required to remove her testicles. Because she ran into so much difficulty getting help with this, in desperation, she came up with an alternative plan to attempt removing them herself, even though she knew she could likely bleed to death.
The desperation to escape either emotional or physical pain or both often causes suicide. The person may be depressed or simply so stressed by pain, they attempt suicide whether or not they fully desire death.

Assisted Suicide

Many times those with a terminal illness wish to die in order to escape a long, painful death from their illness. They may seek an assisted suicide, either from their loved ones or from a doctor.
Palliative care by a hospice doctor can eliminate pain for a dying patient while other hospice workers can help the person say good-bye to their family and friends in a way that helps all sides with the grieving process. It is important that quality hospice care is provided for those who need it. Without the fear of a painful death, most people would choose to bring closure to their relationships before death.

"Suicide by Cop"

A person suffering severe emotional pain may do something to threaten a police officer in order to aggravate the officer to shoot them. This is often called "suicide by cop".
If people knew how to reach out for help without the stigma connected with mental illness, there would be a way for police and others to

help the person acknowledge their need and obtain proper help without the need to aggravate others to kill them. This is why education concerning mental illness and crisis intervention is so important, especially among police officers. Special training is sometimes provided for certain officers in an area so if you have a mental illness or may need to call for help for someone else in a crisis, it is imperative to find out ahead of time which specially trained officers you need to ask for when calling for help from emergency personnel.

Chapter 6 The Seeking Love side

Suicide Attempt
by Judena Klebs

The pills lay on the table
Half-dissolved
And what about my problems?
Were they solved?
What was the cry so urgent from within?
Whose love was I
Through death compelled to win?
I did not know
Nor did I dare consider
The reasons why my life
Was tossed as litter
Why should I try
To analyze
The things my death
Should comprise?
Why should I search the reason
I was bitter?

Though I did not die
I could always try again
What better way to express
My inward pain?
Yet I must stop to think
Just to be sure
That death for me
Would be a final cure
Will someone suggest to me
A better way
While I sort my thoughts
Before the day
Is gone
And I will listen no more?
Will someone enter my life
Before the door
Is closed and all creation cries, "Too late!"
What will it take to turn
My desperate fate?

Compassion, come
And blend your tears with mine
Come, True Respect
And meet me where I pine
Lest, like the dusk
I quietly slip away
Because there were no words
For me to say

If one has been deprived of love in childhood, seeking love wherever
and however it may be found can become a desperate obsession. Love, a
seemingly unattainable thing becomes mysterious in the same way death
is mysterious for those of us alive. The search for love can become
associated with death especially when there is violence and attempts
made on the life of a child.

My own personal experience with this search for love through death was
when at age 13, I became aware of my father trying to smother me in
one of his fits of rage. I had never been able to find a way to please
him or to obtain love from him and after that incident, I thought my
death would please him in a way my life could not and from that time
forth, I became obsessed with thoughts of suicide. I thought perhaps
this would be a way to earn his love at last.

When love is elusive, a person desperate for that love will try any
avenue they think may bring them the comfort of that love. There have
been cases where a suicidal person thinks of death as their "lover" in
an erotic sense. Any type of love can be sought through suicide.

A therapist needs to help a person identify areas of love deprivation
in their life to help them develop positive, life affirming ways to
feel love without associating it with death. It is helpful to work on
new skills in which a person can learn to give and receive love.

Chapter 7 The Fear of Life Side

Those who have experienced a lot of rejection, hurt, or other
suffering especially as children associate life as being made up only
of these unpleasant things. Also those who experience a lot of fear,
either due to trauma or the mental illness of Schizophrenia, which is
many times dominated by paranoia, want to escape these painful things.
To do so, one may "run away" from life. The alternative is to seek
death. Even though death, too, is scary, being the unknown, a person
may be more afraid of life than they are of death.
However, if a person has hope that their life can improve through
psychiatric treatment or more positive experiences, they may keep
trying to get help and to stay alive. New concepts of possibilities
for their life experiences can assist them in obtaining the courage to
keep surviving temptations to suicide.
Counselors who can find ways to instill that hope in someone who
associates life with prolonged suffering by painting a new picture of
what their life can be like can help a person feel that it is worth the
effort to keep themselves alive.
For example, an art therapist can help the person literally draw or
paint a picture of what they want in their life. In this and perhaps
other ways a person can begin to envision a different kind of life
than they have ever known and begin to "dream a new dream" of life
which will begin to take away the fear of life.
Although fear of life is common among those who have suffered in these
ways, another factor that can ironically be a part of suicidal
temptation is a fear of death. Ordinarily, this is a normal fear which
causes us to avoid death but this can become a factor in suicide when
a person who experiences this fear is tired of the foreboding fear of
death itself and wants to get the process of dying over with in order
to solve the mystery and get past the fear.
This problem can be helped by alleviating the fear of death itself
with a healthy understanding of it and a comforting faith in an
afterlife, whether that faith is a Christian one or simply the faith
that we will live on in our contributions to the world after we die.

This poem is from my book, From Rejection to Love:

Suicide

There's a dark world where I can hide
A place that is called "Suicide"
Where no one can touch me or rip my heart
A place to which I long to depart
It seems so safe compared to life
To turn to pills, razor blade, or knife
Even physical pain brings a certain release
From deeper pain and brings me peace
Cut off from friends who seem like foes
Hidden away in the dark where no one knows
The secrets I am afraid to tell
Where no one can get to know me well
Because they might not really love me
If they look in the dark and can somehow see
My past and all it has done to my soul
Suicide is my last control
To choose to live means to open my life
That is worse than pain of death or knife
The risks I take are more painful for me
Than bleeding or dying could ever be
And yet I hear a voice, a call
Wooing me gently away from it all
Saying, "Give us a chance to somehow care.
Come out of the dark and the dangers there."
But if I'm afraid to take your hand
Please, try somehow to understand
That it's safer here in my dark domain
Where I've found my own way to cope with pain
And forgive me for not responding to your call
When I'm able to hear your voice at all
Alone in this dark world I have made
Trying to comfort myself in its silent shade
Yet don't stop calling me out. Please reach your hand to me
There may be a chance that I'll take it, you see
And come out of this world and come out of the night
To grasp on to some hope and continue my fight
A chance that your love will get through some way
And bring me back into the light of day
And I'll have less need to run and hide
To the world that is called "Suicide"

Chapter 8 The Belonging Side

Shawn and Brenda were high school sweethearts. They both wanted to vow their love and loyalty to one another. They also both struggled with depression but tried to cheer each other up.
One day Shawn's best friend, Brian committed suicide and Shawn was devastated. He felt guilt that he may have let Brian down somehow and that he had not been loyal enough to the friendship to allow Brian to die alone.
Finally, in Shawn's grief, he decided that he also should end his own life. He told Brenda how he felt. At first, Brenda tried to talk him out of it but she also felt hopeless and did not want Shawn to die alone. In the end, Shawn and Brenda made a pact to end their lives at the same time and die together.
Sometimes people make such suicide pacts and there have been clusters of suicide, especially among young people often called "copy cat" suicides. These show a need for belonging to another person or group of people to which one feels loyal and with whom one identifies. Unfortunately, this peer pressure can also lead to "daring" others to kill themselves which is a form of bullying. The message communicated from the bully is that suicide is a courageous act. Ironically, people who end their life are often called "cowards".
Because of our self-preservation instinct, suicide is ordinarily a difficult thing to do until other factors over-ride that instinct. It is neither courageous nor cowardly. However, many times it takes more courage to live.
A low sense of belongingness is one great factor in suicide. The way to help solve people's need for belonging is to find a way for them to relate to others in meaningful ways, ways that will provide warm human contact and a family-type atmosphere, especially for those who have not had emotionally healthy families.
Perhaps support groups for those with similar struggles or clubs for those with similar interests could help provide a sense of belongingness, maintaining for them some kind of connections between people. Reaching out to the depressed person through phone calls, cards in the mail, or being available to visit a person who feels cut-off from others is especially important during times when there has been a death of a family member or friend and even more so if that death was by suicide. This could help the grieving person to avoid the feeling that many people experience in times of grief that they should "join" their loved one through suicide.

Chapter 9 The Cry for Help Side

A poem from my book From Rejection to Love:

Beneath The Ground

There is a well of pain
So dark and deep
Beneath the ground
Where willows weep
Filled up with tears
And too far down to see
In the depths
Of the inner parts of me

All alone in there
Are pools of despair
And of grief that cannot reach my face
By the hint of a sigh
Or by a tear that sneaks by
You might sense the slightest trace
Of the pain that's too far down to see
In the depths
Of the inner parts of me

Send down a bucket
Into the well
Bring something to the surface
Allow me to tell
Some of the things I've been afraid to say
Before vines cover the ground
And you can't find a way
To where I am hidden
Too far down to see
In the depths
Of the inner parts of me

"You're only trying to get attention!" Teresa's mother screamed at her.
"Stop threatening suicide!"
"I'm not threatening." Teresa answered,
"I'm trying to tell you I need help."
Teresa had dared to open up to her mother to tell her she felt like
killing herself. She had hoped her mother would somehow help and

comfort her.

"People who talk about it don't really do it anyway.", her mother went on.
Just the opposite of her mother's last comment is true. People often
send out warning signals, trying to get help before ending their
lives.

Let us say that some element of Teresa's suicidal inclinations were to
get her mom's attention. Would that not be because attention is needed
at this time?

All of us need attention and love. If a child does not feel loved,
they may settle for any kind of attention. If we can't get positive
attention, we try for negative attention. Being ignored invalidates us.
If a person has to try suicide in order to get enough attention to
feel significant to others, it is a very desperate way to try to get
one's needs met.

Suicide has long been thought of as a cry for help. It is that and
more. The desperate feelings and deep hurts that push a person toward
suicide tend to make it difficult to reach out for help. If one dares
to express that desperation and are shamed for it, it only adds to the
despair concerning one's self esteem and one's own life.

When someone tells a person that they don't believe that person would
actually attempt suicide, it is no different than the bully daring
someone to try it. Once again, if trying suicide is how someone has to
prove they really mean it, they are definitely desperate enough to be
taken seriously. A person needs compassion and reassurance of love at
this time, not condemnation or judgment. There is nothing wrong in a
person reaching out for help, even if they do it in a way that seems a
manipulative threat. It still needs to be taken seriously. Remember,
anyone who admits suicidal thoughts is desperate for help no matter
how they come across.

There is also a myth that if a suicidal person discusses their suicidal
ideation with others, it will make them more suicidal and also that learning
about others who struggle with suicide will give them more ideas about
how to harm themselves. Just the opposite is true of this as well.
People need to talk about it and identifying with others who struggle
with it helps free them so they don't feel so alone. They need to talk
openly about their temptations and depression in order to free
themselves from the feelings and thoughts.

Just as life flourishes in the sunlight and withers and dies in the
darkness, keeping their struggles secretive and hidden causes the
person to feel more inclined toward suicide. They need to be
encouraged to open up and to share freely their thoughts and feelings
in order to be helped.

Chapter 10 The Justice side

Bradley was a loner. He felt distrustful of the other students at his
high school. When he had dared to be friendly to some of his
classmates, they had rejected him. He felt angry and worthless when
others ignored him or just stared at him without speaking to him.
Bradley had been suffering from long episodes of depression and had
been thinking of suicide for several months. He finally came up with a
plan to sneak his father's gun out of its hiding place and use it to
shoot himself, but he also felt the need to bring "justice" on his
fellow classmates by taking them with him to his death.
The day Bradley took the gun to school and started shooting, he
targeted first the students who had seemed to reject him before
turning the gun on himself. He thought he was doing the "right thing"
by bringing these students to justice.
When the horrified citizens of Bradley's town looked at this tragedy,
they were puzzled that someone like Bradley would do such a thing
because he seemed so quiet and withdrawn and thought he could never
become aggressive enough to commit murder. They were not even aware
that Bradley had been depressed and thinking of ending his own life
months before.
Like in the case of Bradley, most murder-suicides start with a
decision for suicide first, then, after taking matters into one's own
hands, they become both judge and jury to themselves and others,
sentencing all to death. This is not a true justice but one in the
perpetrator's mind.
There are other cases, where family members are involved that are seen
by the suicidal person as a "mercy killing" or a duty because there is
the belief that the family members either could not or would not want
to make it on their own after the person's death, so they are
destroyed as well.
Even in the case of suicide bombers, there is evidence of suicidal
depression involved in the bomber's life. Then, combined with
religious teachings that it is their duty to bring judgment on others,
they choose to die a "heroic martyr's" death, which brings a kind of
glory to their suicide.
Because the primary motive in a murder-suicide is first suicide
itself, that is the place to start in preventing these tragedies. To
detect the decision for suicide which could also lead to murder, a
clinician may observe some of these signs:

1) Agitation
2) Insomnia
3)Nightmares

4) Social Withdrawal
5) Far-away Stare, often without blinking, and
6) Sudden Weight Loss.

Often a person will not admit to suicidal or homicidal thoughts but if the clinician can get them talking about things on their mind, they may note themes, such as honor, duty or justice coming up. Of course, any underlying mental illness needs to be treated. By saving the life of a would-be suicide, many others lives may be saved as well!

Chapter 11 The Self-Harm Side

Anita would often feel upset and not know how to express her feelings.
She learned that harming herself distracted her from her emotional
pain. She would cut on her arms and legs, burn herself at times, and
bang her head as well as other types of self-harm. She would always
carefully cover up the evidence of these self-injuries. She would
express her pain to herself since she felt others could not understand
her feelings.
Most of the time, Anita's cutting was relatively minor and not life
threatening. However, at times she was tempted to injure herself more
seriously. She thought about suicide at times when she was depressed.
Just as self-harm is a way to cope with emotional pain and may or may
not be with the intent to die, suicide itself expresses deep emotional
pain. In my own experience, at times I thought that making myself bleed
"enough" might help me "wash the hurt out of my heart". It was an
irrational fantasy I had because of the severe agony I experienced in
my emotional realm.
Self-harm is common in those who have been taught not to express
strong emotions. Shame, anger, and self-disgust are turned onto one's
self.
Only a psychiatric professional can provide diagnosis and treatment
for someone who self-injures. There are treatments which are helpful,
including medication, cognitive/behavioral therapy, and interpersonal
therapy which assists people in gaining insights and skills to develop
and maintain relationships.

Chapter 12 The Punishment Side

Aaron was raised in a strict Fundamentalist church. The preacher often
warned about the judgments of an eternal hell for sinners. Aaron felt he
could do nothing right and thought that if God was going to judge anyone,
it would surely be him!
After going through some trauma and depression in his life, Aaron felt
even worse. He thought that if he took himself out of this world, he
could keep from leading others astray by his example and at least save
them from the punishments of hell which he felt that he, alone,
deserved.
When Aaron finally told his parents that he wanted to die and was
thinking of suicide, they tried to scare him out of it by telling him
that God could never forgive him if he did that. This made him feel
even more ashamed and convinced him further that he needed to be
punished in hell. Finally, Aaron decided that he should help God
punish him by punishing himself and he ended his life.
Guilt, shame, condemnation, and punishment do not free a person from
suicide. They only add to an already miserable set of feelings. Trying
to frighten a person out of suicide only destroys what little bit of
self-esteem they may have left.
Historically, before mental illness was beginning to be understood a
little, the suicide's body was punished as an example to others not to
commit this sin. Their families were also punished and then as now,
the suicide is not allowed to be buried in some Christian and Jewish
cemeteries.
Shame, punishment, and hopelessness are heaped upon suicidal people in
churches, books, and everyday talk. It is said to be selfish, sinful,
and cowardly. Perhaps the way we phrase the words, "commit suicide"
makes it sound like a crime rather than an illness. For this reason,
some prefer to use the phrase, "die by suicide" to clarify it and put
it in a category with other illnesses.

Chapter 13 The Symbolic Side

Louise remembered being weaned from the breast as a toddler. About the same time, she remembered that her mother also failed to give her much affection from that time on as she was growing older. Besides this rejection, an accumulation of other factors had led her to experience depression as she grew up.
Whenever Louise began to feel depressed to the point of suicidal thoughts, she imagined drinking poison or overdosing on her medication. An oral method of suicide would always stand out in her mind. Could this be related to the withdrawal of love from her mother at the same time as her weaning?
Samuel was lonely. He felt the coldness of other people in his life toward him. If only he could find warmth and understanding from the people in his life!
At times of despair, Samuel thought about setting himself on fire. Could this have to do with the warmth he craved?
Doris wanted someone to persist in loving her and not drift away out of her life so easily. She longed to be overpowered with a strong love in her life. When she became despondent, she imagined throwing herself in front of a train so she could at least be overpowered by something in her death.
Although the methods chosen by suicide victims to destroy themselves are sometimes due to their availability or to the degree that they are lethal, sometimes they are chosen by what they symbolize to the subconscious mind. When our conscious mind can tap into the subconscious mind we can learn a lot about the needs we are trying to meet. When helping a suicidal person, it may help to explore with them their choices of certain methods. When it can be identified which needs they are trying to meet in their life, those can be replaced with true answers rather than suicidal alternatives.
If you are a person who struggles with suicide, are there particular methods which tend to present themselves to you? With the help of a therapist, perhaps you can examine what needs in your life you are trying to meet.

Chapter 14 The Intervention Side

Jenny ran away from the mental hospital because she felt as though she
wanted to die and she did not understand why the hospital protected
her from her suicidal gestures. She had lost hope in getting the help
she needed and thought about throwing herself into heavy traffic.
Jenny had tried to run away before and instead of receiving compassion
and understanding from the staff people who caught her, she was
scolded. This time, though, while hiding and trying to make a final
decision about her suicide plan, a staff person named Ron, who was out
looking for her gently approached her when he found her because he
could see that she was frightened. Instead of yelling at Jenny for
running away, he spoke to her kindly and was finally able to coax her
to go back with him to the safety of the hospital.
When intervening in a suicidal crisis:
1) Show total acceptance. Don't scold but be sensitive to how the person is
feeling. They are frightened because there is always some degree of
ambivalence about whether they are making the right decision to end their
life.
2) No sudden moves. Be gentle. Although, if a weapon is involved, you
may want to snatch it away from them as soon as possible, it is better if
you can get them to hand it over willingly. Remember that in some ways, a
weapon may feel like a "security blanket" to a suicidal person because it
represents their ticket out of an unbearable life. Your sudden movement
may come across as aggressive and threatening, causing them to become
combative.
3) Listen Actively. Help the person to express their feelings and reflect
back to them what you think they are saying, continuing to ask questions
to help them fully express what is bothering them.
4) Instill hope by helping the person explore options. The suicidal person
has "tunnel vision" and can see only suicide as the way out of their
problems.
5) Provide support in getting further help for the person.

Here is another poem from my book "From Rejection to Love":

Tender Heart

It is your tender heart I'm needing
Your tender heart I'm longing for
When my soul is filled with grief
And my mind is filled with war
It's not your cleverness or intellect
Nor impressive words that you could say
But your soft and gentle touch
And your kind and caring way
There are no answers or solutions
That a friend could ever give
That could take the place of the love they share
And the life they help you live
So when sorrow overwhelms me
And you take me by the hand
I need your caring and compassion
Even when you don't understand
'Cause it's your tender heart that heals me
And lifts the burden that I bear
It holds me close and shields me
Showing me you really care
Your tender heart prepares me
To respond in loving ways
When it soothes and relieves me
On my tormenting, painful days
So let your tender heart be ready
To receive my love too
Because you will learn as time continues
That I have a tender heart for you

Chapter 15 The Prevention Side

George was feeling hopeless and depressed. He knew he should try to
reach out for help to someone instead of acting on his suicidal
thoughts. However, he owned a gun and knew how to use it. How easy it
would be to just pull the trigger and get rid of all his deep sadness
and hurt! The temptation was too great to get this all over with
instead of taking the time to think all his agony through or to dare
to trust someone else with his problems. Why go on any longer with the
gun so near at hand?

Denise stood at the top of a bridge. how easy it would be to step over
the edge and end her difficult life! She was not completely sure she
wanted to go through with it but there was no one to talk to in order
to work through her feelings. If there were anyone or anything to hold
her back, she might reconsider but she was all alone on the bridge
with her painful thoughts and ready to throw all restraints away that
were still inside of her.

What if George had no access to a gun during his depressed episodes?
What are the chances he might reach out and get help?

What if there were barricades on that high bridge so that it would not
be so easy for Denise to leap to her death? What if there were
counselors regularly patrolling some high bridges that are famous for
suicide? Or perhaps phone booths that automatically could dial a
suicide hot-line? Would this possibly give Denise time to reconsider
and seek help?

What if, each time the media reports a suicide, they acknowledge that
the person had some type of mental disorder that is treatable? What if
they listed local services where help can be found?

What if many people were regularly trained to recognize the symptoms
of suicide risks in their daily interactions with people? What if they
could provide human contact and support for those near suicide?

The American Association of Suicidology has a mnemonic for suicide
warning signs: IS PATH WARM?

I-Ideation
S-Substance Abuse

P-Purposelessness
A-Anxiety and Agitation
T-Trapped Feelings
H-Hopelessness

W-Withdrawal
A-Anger
R-Recklessness
M-Mood Fluctuation

Note:After many years with concerned citizens advocating for changes,
some have been implemented at the Golden Gate Bridge at San Francisco,
California. There is now a course web of steel being constructed under
the bridge called a "suicide net". to catch jumpers. Also, phone
stations are in place for crisis calls. We need to keep advocating for
many more improvements to be made everywhere in suicide prevention.

Chapter 16 The Grief Side

11-year-old Jasmine was my violin student. One day she came to her
scheduled lesson with a very serious look on her face. I knew
something was wrong. Then she proceeded to tell me her story, which
began a very sad adventure for me in trying to comfort her and her
mother through a time of grief.
Jasmine told me that her father had killed himself just the day before
while she was home alone with him. She told me that when she woke up
in the morning, she went through the house looking for him and found
his dead body, had screamed and ran over to the neighbor's house, who
called the police.
Although Jasmine had just been through this trauma the day before, she
had insisted on coming to her lesson and being the one to tell me,
herself, what had happened. Of course, I was in shock and I told her
she did not need to do her lesson that day if she did not feel up to
it. She still insisted on proceeding with her lesson.
The next couple of years, while doing everything I knew to do to help
Jasmine and her mother through this difficult time, I witnessed their
struggles and observed other people's reaction to this tragedy. Some
of the reactions of others to this family's grief showed me that
society still has a long way to go in handling the aftermath of
suicide.
Suicide causes more than just a normal kind of grief. Instead the
grief is complicated by a whole set of reactions. One of these
reactions is a guilt/blame cycle that can continue on and on.
I noticed that Jasmine went from blaming herself for not waking up in
time to stop the suicide to blaming her Dad's employer for putting him
under too much pressure to blaming her father for his own suicide.
There are some reasons these tendencies to blame are inaccurate
conclusions.
First, blaming ourselves for not being able to stop the suicide
assumes we are omnipotent. Secondly, we can never be sure of all the
influences of others that contributed to the person's decision to end
their life. Thirdly, It does not take into account the fact that
suicide is the manifestation of an illness that can cause death like
any other disease.
It is unproductive to get caught in this guilt/blame cycle. Instead,
every member of the family needs a chance to grieve in their own way
while receiving emotional support. Both individual and family therapy
are essential, as well as suicide survivor's support groups. Friends
need to provide compassion and sensitivity, which includes listening
without judging.
History tells us that for a long time in the past, families would be

punished for the suicide of their loved ones. They were shamed and not allowed to inherit from the deceased but instead left destitute.

To some extent, society still punishes the families of suicide victims because of the taboos and stigma surrounding suicide. For others to blame any member of the family, including blaming the person who took their own life because it is supposedly "selfish" only adds to everyone's pain and grief.

It is helpful for those grieving a suicide to be aware that suicide is neither a rejection nor a lack of love from the deceased. Even if there had been expressions of anger or threats manifested before the death, there is rarely any element of vengeance involved in suicide. Rather than deliberately trying to hurt anyone, the person more than likely falsely saw themselves as a burden and were under a delusion that they were doing everyone a favor.

Conclusion

May we learn to look at the big picture concerning suicide.

May each suicidal person we contact find help and hope.

May we all do our part to save lives and to comfort the mourning.

And may we walk in all the new light being shed on this greatly misunderstood subject, helping to educate others along our journey.

Resources

National Suicide Prevention Lifeline
1-800-273-8255
(will be shortened to 988 in the future)
https://suicidepreventionlifeline.org/

The Gay, Lesbian, Bisexual and Transgender National Hotline
1-888-843-4564
http://www.glbthotline.org/hotline.html

Trevor Lifeline for LGBTQ Youth
1-866-488-7386
https://www.thetrevorproject.org/